EMBRACE OF THOUGHT

POETRY OF THE MIND'S QUIET EXPLORATION

SUBHASMITA PANDA.

Made with ♥ on the Notion Press Platform
www.notionpress.com

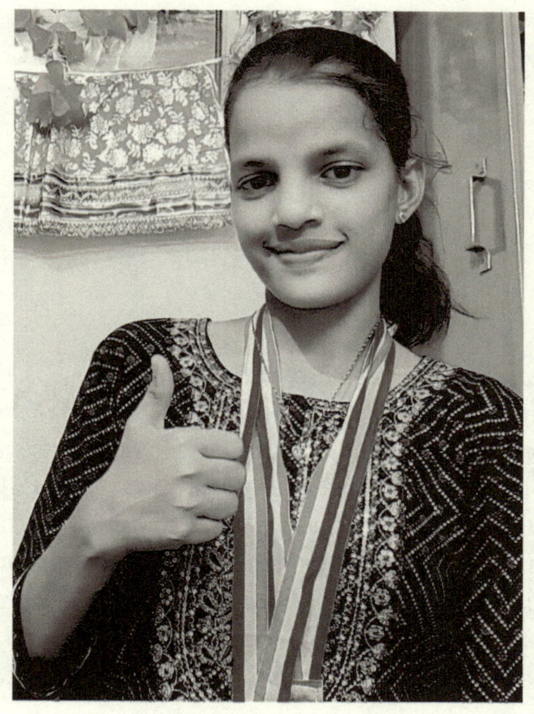

SUBHASMITA PANDA

*"**To** the seekers of inner peace, the dreamers of quiet worlds, and the explorers of thought's vast terrain. This book is dedicated to those who understand that true discovery often lies in the silence between words, in the spaces where the mind wanders free. May these poems serve as a guide through the delicate pathways of the heart and mind, embracing the subtle yet profound beauty of quiet exploration. For in the silence of thought, we come to*

know ourselves better, uncovering truths that are as elusive as they are timeless. To everyone who believes in the magic of words and the depth of unspoken emotions, this book is for you. It is a tribute to the thinkers who ponder life's questions and the dreamers who see endless possibilities. Thank you for opening these pages and allowing my thoughts to find a home in your heart. May this collection bring you moments of comfort, inspiration, and connection, as it reflects the shared human experience in all its beauty and complexity."

Contents

Contents

Contents

* A Journey Begins *

"Come, let us explore the beauty of fleeting moments captured in timeless words."

"Welcome to a world where words hold magic and emotions take flight. Within these pages, each poem invites you to explore the depths of feeling, thought, and imagination. Let the rhythm of the verses guide you, and may you find a reflection of your own heart in every line. Open these pages and let the rhythm of words guide you on a journey through the heart, the mind, and the soul. Each page carries a whisper of the universe, waiting for your heart to listen and your soul to dance along."

Foreword

Poetry is the language of the soul—a bridge between the unspoken and the understood, the ordinary and the profound. "**Embrace of Thought: Poetry of Mind's Quiet Exploration**" invites readers on a contemplative journey, weaving words into an intricate tapestry of emotion, reflection, and discovery.

In a world often consumed by noise and haste, these poems serve as gentle whispers of introspection. They delve into the quiet corners of the mind where ideas take root, where dreams simmer, and where the heart dares to question and feel. Each verse is a portal to moments of stillness and wonder, capturing fleeting thoughts and grounding them in the permanence of ink.

This collection is not merely a record of musings; it is an exploration—a dialogue with the self, the universe, and the intricate dance between the two. As you turn these pages, may you find solace in the familiarity of shared human experiences and inspiration to embark on your own quiet explorations.

Let this be more than a book. Let it be a companion, a mirror, and a spark for your own embrace of thought. Welcome to the poetry of the mind's quiet exploration.

Prologue

Within the vast landscape of the human mind lies a quiet sanctuary—a place where thoughts bloom unrestrained, where emotions flow like rivers carving their path through time. "Embrace of Thought: Poetry of Mind's Quiet Exploration" is an invitation to wander through that sanctuary, to sit in the stillness and listen to the gentle rustle of unspoken words.

These poems are not just creations; they are journeys—little lanterns illuminating the hidden corridors of introspection. Each verse is a brushstroke on the canvas of existence, capturing fleeting moments, unvoiced emotions, and the silent conversations we often have with ourselves.

This book does not demand to be read; it asks to be felt. It invites you to pause, breathe, and discover the extraordinary in the ordinary. It is a celebration of the whispers that guide us, the reflections that shape us, and the questions that keep us searching.

Let this prologue be the opening of a door—a step into a world where words embrace thoughts and quiet exploration becomes a voyage of connection and understanding. The journey ahead is not only mine but also yours, for these poems live in the shared spaces of our humanity. Welcome to the embrace of thought. Let us begin.

Acknowledgements

I extend my heartfelt thanks to those who have been a part of this quiet yet profound journey. To the stillness of my own mind, which has been both a sanctuary and a wellspring of creativity, I owe the essence of these poems. The silence between words, the soft whisper of thought, and the moments of introspection are the foundation upon which this book is built.

My deepest gratitude goes to the readers who dare to venture into these spaces of silence, embracing the subtlety and depth of thought's quiet exploration. You are the true companions in this journey. I also wish to acknowledge the unwavering support of my loved ones, whose understanding, encouragement, and belief in my voice have kept me grounded through the challenges of this endeavor. May this book serve as an invitation to others to pause, listen, and embrace the peace found within their own minds."

Every poem in this collection is a seed nurtured by the rich soil of experiences, the gentle rain of inspiration, and the sunlight of encouragement from those who have touched my life. This book, "Embrace of Thought: Poetry of Mind's Quiet Exploration," is as much yours as it is mine.

To the quiet moments that whispered truths and the chaotic ones that demanded attention—thank you for shaping the words that now bloom on these pages. To my family, whose unwavering love and belief have been the roots grounding my creativity, and to my friends, whose kind words were the breeze that stirred these thoughts into expression, I am deeply grateful.

To the great poets of the past and the everyday storytellers of the present, your voices have been the echoes guiding my own. To nature, the eternal muse, thank you for your boundless beauty and the wisdom you impart in silence.And most of all, to you—the reader. You are the soul of this book, the reason these words hold meaning. For embracing these thoughts with your own, for exploring these quiet reflections with an open heart, thank you for completing this journey.

This book stands as a fruit of collaboration between the seen and the unseen, the spoken and the felt. May its essence inspire you as deeply as your presence inspires me.

Preface

Poetry has always been my sanctuary, a place where thoughts take flight and emotions find their voice. **"Embrace of Thought: Poetry of Mind's Quiet Exploration"** is born out of my longing to pause and reflect, to listen to the whispers of the mind and the echoes of the heart.

This collection is a journey into introspection—a delicate dance between the conscious and the subconscious, where silence speaks louder than words and simplicity reveals its depth. Each poem represents a moment of stillness, a fragment of curiosity, or a spark of insight that emerged from the quiet exploration of my own thoughts.

In these verses, you may find traces of joy, sorrow, hope, and wonder. Some may resonate like a familiar melody; others may invite you to see the world from a different perspective. This book is not about answers but about questions, not about conclusions but about journeys.

It is my hope that as you read these poems, you too will find moments of connection, inspiration, and reflection. Whether you seek solace in solitude or a companion for your own musings, may this collection offer a comforting embrace to your thoughts.

Thank you for joining me on this exploration of the mind's quiet landscapes.

With gratitude and love,
Subhasmita Panda.

CHAPTER ONE

" What Is Poetry? "

"*It's the voice of the heart, a song of the soul,*
A canvas of words where emotions unfold.
A rhythm, a dance, a melody untamed,
A spark of the spirit that cannot be named."

"*It's laughter and tears, the whispers of rain,*
The echo of joy, the shadow of pain.
A bridge to the timeless, a key to the lost,
A flame that burns bright, no matter the cost."

"*Poetry lives where silence resides,*
In the depths of the ocean, the turn of the tides.
It's life distilled to its essence, its core,
A language of beauty, forever and more."

CHAPTER TWO

" WHO AM I? "

"*I am the whisper of dawn's first light,*
The shadow that dances with fading night.
I am the flame that refuses to die,
A question unspoken, a wondering "Why?""

"*I am the roots that dig deep in the earth,*
The echoes of dreams that gave me birth.
I am the storm and the calm that remains,
The river that carves through mountains and plains."

"*I am the laughter, the tears, the unknown,*
The seeds of the future in fields I've sown.
I am the mirror of all I create,
The architect shaping my destined fate."

"*I am the spark that ignites the new,*
A prism of colors in every hue.
I am not fixed, I rise and I fall,
A fragment, a story, the whole of it all."

"*I am the voice of my truth's refrain,*
The freedom found through joy and pain.
I am the path, the journey, the guide,

SUBHASMITA PANDA.

The boundless spirit that lives inside."

CHAPTER THREE

* THE POET WITHIN *

"A heart that whispers, a mind that dreams,
Words flowing softly in vibrant streams.
A weaver of thoughts, both light and deep,
Through ink and paper, memories seep."

"The stars and shadows, the sun and rain,
All fuel the fire that dances in vain.
For a poet's soul, forever awake,
Turns life's whispers into songs that ache."

"To touch the world with a gentle pen,
Binding hearts now and again.
A poet's craft, pure and true,
The world unfolds—all through you."

CHAPTER FOUR

* THE WRITER *

"A writer sits with pen in hand,
In the quiet of a room so grand,
Their mind a maze of thoughts untold,
A universe of dreams unfolds."

"Words like rivers flow with grace,
Each sentence finds its destined place,
A world appears from ink and page,
Where silence speaks, and hearts engage."

"They weave the fabric of the mind,
A tapestry of worlds to find,
The truth they seek in black and white,
While dancing with the shades of night."

"A writer's work is never done,
For stories live beyond the sun,
And when the ink begins to fade,
A new adventure is remade."

"In quiet hours, they come alive,
Through words, the soul will always thrive.
For writers write not just to tell,

But to unlock the deepest spell."

CHAPTER FIVE

* I RISE *

"I rise, with the strength of my past,
A heritage that's built to last.
From the roots of my ancestors deep,
I rise, their wisdom I keep."

"I rise, with the stories they've told,
Of courage and love, both brave and bold.
In their footsteps, I find my way,
I rise with pride each new day."

"I rise, carrying their dreams on my back,
A legacy strong, no path I lack.
From their struggles, I draw my power,
I rise, like a blooming flower."

"I rise, honoring what came before,
A heritage that opens the door.
With every step, I stand tall and free,
I rise, and forever I will be."

"I rise, like the sun in the sky,
From the dark, I spread my wings and fly.
Step by step, I climb up high,

No matter how hard, I still try."

"I rise, like the waves in the sea,
Strong and free, just like me.
Even when the storm is near,
I rise above and face my fear."

"I rise, no matter what comes my way,
With every fall, I stand up and say,
I'm not giving up, I won't back down,
I rise, I rise, I wear my crown."

"I rise, because I know I can,
With hope in my heart and strength in my hands.
I rise, and I will not stop,
For I am strong, and I will reach the top."

CHAPTER SIX

* LET'S BEGIN *

"A blank page whispers, soft and clear,
A canvas waiting, a world to appear.
No need for perfection, no need for haste,
Each word a seed, no thought a waste."

"The dawn of a journey, the edge of the stream,
Where reality bends to the will of a dream.
Courage awakens, doubt falls away,
The first step forward births the day."

"Let's begin with a spark, a flicker, a start,
A brush of the mind, a beat of the heart.
For every beginning holds the key,
To what could become, to what might be."

"Let's begin with wonder, with open eyes,
With questions that stretch to endless skies.
Each stumble, a lesson; each pause, a song,
The rhythm of progress steady and strong."

"The end is unknown, the path unwritten,
But the soul is eager, the spirit smitten.
With hope as our guide, the stars as our kin,

Take my hand, my friend—let's begin."

CHAPTER SEVEN

THE SONG OF LIFE

"***Music*** *flows, a river wide,*
A melody where hearts can hide.
It whispers softly, then it roars,
Unlocking dreams behind closed doors."

"*Each note a story, pure, profound,*
A language where no words are found.
It lifts us up, it pulls us down,
A dance of joy, a softened frown."

"*In every beat, a rhythm beats,*
A heartbeat shared in gentle feats.
It carries us through joy and pain,
And in its arms, we rise again."

"*The strings, the keys, the drums, the voice,*
Together, making hearts rejoice.
For music is the soul's embrace,
A timeless gift, a sacred grace."

"*So let it play, let it ignite,*
The spark of love, the fire of light.
For in the song, we are set free,

In music, we are truly we."

CHAPTER EIGHT

* THE PATH OF LIFE *

"***In*** *the quiet hush of morning's glow,*
A single path begins to show.
It winds and bends, both sharp and wide,
A journey taken with no guide."

"*One step, just one, is all it takes,*
To set the course, to bridge the lakes,
Of doubt, of fear, of days unknown,
A road to tread, yet not alone."

"*For every step that marks the way,*
A choice is made, a role to play.
The road ahead, though still unseen,
Is shaped by what we've yet to dream."

"*In moments when the world stands still,*
We find our strength, we shape our will.
Through hardships, joy, through rain and sun,
The path ahead is never done."

"*One way, one choice, defines the day,*
And from it, life begins to sway.
The road may change, but we remain,

The architects of joy and pain."

"Each footfall echoes in the soul,
A testament to making whole
The journey that begins anew,
With every choice that we pursue."

CHAPTER NINE

* Two Legs, Two Hands *

"***With*** *two legs, I stand so tall,*
Stepping forward, I rise, I fall.
Each stride a journey, wide and grand,
I walk through life with strength to stand."

"*With two hands, I reach the sky,*
I build, I touch, I lift, I try.
They shape my world, they hold my dreams,
In every touch, a new hope gleams."

"*Two legs to move, to roam, to chase,*
Two hands to hold, to carve, to grace.
Together they guide me through each day,
In every step, they light my way."

"*Two legs, two hands, a gift so true,*
A strength that helps me see things through.
For with these parts, both strong and kind,
The world is mine, the future I'll find."

CHAPTER TEN

* TUBE LIGHT OF LIFE *

*"**In** the stillness of the darkened room,*
A flicker stirs, dispels the gloom,
The tubelight hums a quiet tune,
A fragile glow beneath the moon."

"Its beam is soft, yet steady bright,
A symbol in the endless night,
For life, too, glows with moments small,
That guide us through when shadows call."

"At times it flickers, dims, and fades,
Lost in the dark of passing days,
But patience in the quiet stays,
Until it shines through thickest haze."

"Like life itself, it burns so slow,
Yet in its light, we come to know,
That though the path may twist and bend,
The tubelight's glow will never end."

"So let us trust, in darkest times,
That light will come through silent chimes,
For life, like light, will always find
A way to heal, to soothe, remind."

CHAPTER ELEVEN

* A Step Towards Death *

"A single step, so soft, so still,
The hush of time, against my will,
A path unseen, where shadows lie,
Where whispers of the past float by."

"I feel the weight, a quiet pull,
An unseen hand, serene, yet full.
The earth beneath, both warm and cold,
Tells tales of lives that once were bold."

"The wind, it carries ancient sighs,
Of fleeting moments, fading skies,
I take the step, no fear, no fight,
Into the stillness, out of light."

"What lies ahead, I cannot know,
But in this pause, I let it go.
The end is close, but not yet here,
A step towards death, without the fear."

"For death, she waits, a lover's glance,
A tender step, a silent dance,
And though the road may twist and bend,
I find in death, a peaceful friend."

"So onward now, I gently tread,
With every step, a thought, a thread,
And when the final step I take,
I'll rest, at last, for my soul's sake."

CHAPTER TWELVE

The Eyes That See

*"**In** the silence, they softly gleam,*
Two windows open to a dream.
With every glance, they seek, they find,
The beauty hidden deep behind."

"Through the eyes, the world unfolds,
A thousand stories yet untold.
They see the colors, dark and bright,
Reflecting joy, and capturing light."

"They hold the sorrow, the joy, the pain,
The laughter, tears, the sun, the rain.
In every blink, a tale is spun,
Of everything we've lost or won."

"Eyes are mirrors of the soul,
They show our hearts, they make us whole.
With every glance, they speak the truth,
A silent song, a sacred proof."

"So let us cherish what they see,
The wonders of our world, so free.
For in the eyes, the heart can trace

The beauty of the human race."

CHAPTER THIRTEEN

* Never Give Up *

*"**When** shadows loom and hearts grow faint,*
When hope feels weak, and dreams are late,
Hold on, dear soul, through darkest skies,
For after storms, the sun will rise."

"In moments where the road feels steep,
And all you want is just to sleep,
Remember this — the night will pass,
And in its wake, your strength will last."

"Though challenges may block your way,
And doubts whisper at the break of day,
Each step, though small, will lead you through,
A path where dreams come into view."

"So never let the fear take hold,
Or let your spirit be bought or sold.
In every fall, there's strength to find,
A reason to push forward, kind."

"The road is long, the fight is real,
But never give up — it's yours to steal.
For in the end, the prize is clear:

The courage to rise and persevere. ”

“*With every tear, with every scar,*
You've journeyed further than you are.
And though it seems you've lost your way,
The victory's found in what you say: ”

“*I won't give up, I'll rise again,*
Through trials, I'll always ascend.
For deep within, your power's found,
And with each step, you'll leave the ground. ”

“*So stand, take heart, and look ahead,*
For those who rise are never dead.
With every dawn, your soul will sing:
You are the light, you are the king. ”

“***Never give up. Keep moving on.*
*The darkest night precedes the dawn.*** ”

CHAPTER FOURTEEN

* Dreams and Struggles *

"We dream and walk on the path of dreams,
Chasing hope in the rhythm of life's schemes.
But this path is filled with struggles,
Where every step brings challenges and troubles."

"Why dream if there's no struggle?
Life's truth is found in struggle's humble.
Just keep trying, why fear to fail?
If hope remains in your heart, success will sail."

"Slowly, steadily, continue the way,
Embrace the pain that comes to stay.
That's when success will surely arrive,
It's the foundation where you'll thrive."

"Dreams are good, and hope is bright,
Struggles are the way to rise to new heights.
In this journey, as we strive and fight,
Hope's light will shine with all its might."

CHAPTER FIFTEEN

* THE DIVINE PRESENCE OF JAGANNATH *

*"**In** the heart of the sacred land,*
Where rivers flow and temples stand,
A deity, both fierce and kind,
Awaits the worship of the mind."

"Jagannath, the Lord of the Sea,
With eyes of mercy, wild and free,
A chariot drawn by boundless love,
He watches from His throne above."

"His form, a mystery, yet so clear,
In every heart, both far and near,
Carved in wood, a timeless grace,
Radiates peace from His blessed face."

"The waves may roar, the winds may howl,
But Jagannath stands, both pure and proud.
A lord of justice, a lord of light,

Guiding souls through darkest night."

"The Rath Yatra, a pilgrimage grand,
With chants and prayers across the land,
The drums that beat, the flags that fly,
Raise their voices to the sky."

"O Lord, O Jagannath, divine,
In Your presence, we intertwine.
Let Your blessings ever flow,
Through every heart, to let love grow."

"In Your name, we find our way,
Through the night, into the day.
Jagannath, our constant guide,
In You, we live, in You, we abide."

CHAPTER SIXTEEN

* Democracy's Voice *

"**In** *every heart, a spark does glow,*
A voice that speaks, a seed to sow.
In freedom's soil, the roots take hold,
A story of the brave and bold."

"*Where many hands together reach,*
To shape a world that each can teach.
Through open doors and skies so wide,
Democracy, our constant guide."

"*Not a crown, nor single hand,*
But the will of all across the land.
In ballots cast, in choices made,
A union of hopes, a dream portrayed."

"*The power lies within our grasp,*
In peaceful votes, in voices rasp.
From quiet streets to towering spires,
Democracy, what it inspires."

"The right to speak, the right to stand,
A voice united, across the land.
Though paths may twist, and winds may sway,
In unity, we find our way."

"So let us cherish, let us fight,
For the freedoms we hold tight.
For democracy is not a prize,
But a promise in every sunrise."

CHAPTER SEVENTEEN

* MAA: FROM BIRTH TO TODAY *

"From the first cry that broke the silent night,
You held me close, your arms my light.
A bond unspoken, a love so vast,
The roots of my life, in your care cast."

"You taught me to walk, to speak, to dream,
To chase the stars, to follow the stream.
Through scraped knees and endless fears,
You kissed away my falling tears."

"Your lap, my haven, my world so small,
In your stories, I learned to stand tall.
Each sleepless night, each gentle song,
Your sacrifices carried me along."

"As years unfurled, and I grew away,
You stayed my anchor, my guiding ray.
Through youth's rebellion, life's unsure tread,
You whispered wisdom in all you said."

"Now in this era, as time moves on,
I see the battles you've quietly won.
Lines on your face, stories they tell,
Of love and courage you wore so well."

"Maa, you're the thread that weaves my days,
Through every journey, your spirit stays.
From the birth of me to this very hour,
You are my strength, my eternal power."

"No words suffice, no tribute too grand,
To thank the touch of your gentle hand.
Maa, you're my world, my heart, my song,
With you beside me, I'll always belong."

CHAPTER EIGHTEEN

* DEDICATION OF A FATHER *

"A father's love, so steady, true,
A constant force in all he'd do.
With every step, he gave his all,
To catch us when we start to fall."

"Through sleepless nights, and days so long,
He taught us right, he made us strong.
In silence, he would sacrifice,
To give us dreams, to make them rise."

"His hands were worn, but still they held
The hope he knew would soon be swelled.
In every struggle, every fight,
He gave his strength, he shared his light."

"A father's heart, both fierce and kind,
A guiding star, forever blind
To the limits others place on him,
His love, a flame that won't grow dim."

"No crown he wore, no grand applause,
Yet through it all, he stayed the cause.
His legacy, not in a name,
But in the hearts he helped to flame."

"For in the quiet of each day,
A father's work, the price he'd pay,
Is found in all the lives he touched,
In every hug, in every clutch."

"And though his journey might be long,
His love, forever, will stay strong."

CHAPTER NINETEEN

* The Soul of a Girl *

"Beneath the surface, quiet, still,
Where shadows play and time stands still,
There lives a soul, a soft refrain,
A melody born from joy and pain."

"Her heart is an echo of the moon's soft light,
A dancing flame in the depths of night.
She weaves her dreams on winds that sing,
A tapestry, a delicate wing."

"Her soul is like a river's song,
Flowing deep, forever strong.
Each drop a secret, each curve a grace,
Her spirit holds an untold place."

"Through every laugh, through every tear,
A thousand voices whisper near—
The echoes of ancestors, the songs of old,
In the rhythm of her pulse, the stories unfold."

"She's both the storm and the still,
The quiet meadow, the jagged hill.
A spark that ignites the stars above,
A tender touch, the gift of love."

"Her eyes are windows to the skies,
Where dreams take shape and wisdom flies.
In every glance, a thousand tales,
Of untold journeys, of wind and sails."

"Her soul, a secret garden's bloom,
Filling the world with sweet perfume.
It holds the strength of endless seas,
And the quiet hush of winter's breeze."

"A girl—yet more, in essence grand,
A soul that carries time's own hand.
She is both the dawn and the dusk,
A story written in stardust, trust."

"For the soul of a girl is wild and free,
It speaks in the language of eternity.
And though her journey may twist and curl,
It always returns, for she is the world."

CHAPTER TWENTY

* CLASS ROOM *

*"**In** the classroom, quiet and bright,*
Ideas bloom, take silent flight.
Chalk on board and books in hand,
A world of learning, vast and grand."

"The teacher speaks, the students hear,
Questions spark, both far and near.
Each desk a place where minds take root,
A garden of knowledge, fresh and mute."

"The walls may echo with a sigh,
As hands reach up to touch the sky.
Every answer, every thought,
A thread that binds the lessons taught."

"In this space, we rise and fall,
Together growing, learning all.
From every lesson, big and small,
We find our voice, we stand tall."

"In the classroom, dreams unfold,
Stories of the young and bold.
A place where futures find their way,

And knowledge shines, bright as day."

CHAPTER TWENTY-ONE

* SILENT SOUL *

*"**In** the stillness of the midnight air,*
A silent soul, beyond compare,
It drifts like whispers in the breeze,
A quiet heart at perfect ease."

"No need for words, no loud refrain,
Its depth is felt in softest rain,
In spaces where the shadows grow,
The silent soul begins to glow."

"It speaks in silence, calm and clear,
A language only hearts can hear,
A gentle touch, a knowing glance,
It moves in quiet, steady dance."

"Though the world may rush and roar,
It stands unmoved upon the shore,
A peaceful light, a steady flame,
The silent soul will stay the same."

"In every pause, it finds its place,
A timeless dance, a steady grace,
For silence holds the truest sound,

Where all is lost and all is found."

CHAPTER TWENTY-TWO

* THE JOURNEY OF A SINGLE TEAR *

"A single tear, so small, so pure,
A fleeting drop, a heart's allure,
From deep within the soul it springs,
An echo of unspoken things."

"It dances gently, soft and slow,
A whisper of a tale below,
A story told without a word,
A silence that can still be heard."

"It travels down the cheek, a line,
A crystal path through which hearts shine,
A symbol of the pain concealed,
The hopes and dreams that life has healed."

"Beneath the eyes, a well of grief,
A tear becomes a quiet thief,
It steals the weight, the burdened heart,
And lets the soul once more depart."

"For every tear, a sorrow lives,
A life that loss and love forgives,
Yet in its fall, there lies the grace,
A cleansing that time cannot erase."

" It carries with it memories,
Of moments lost, of cherished pleas,
Of laughter shared, of hands once held,
And stories that were never spelled."

"It might be born from joy or pain,
From love that's lost or love that's gained,
A testament to all we feel,
A truth too deep for words to heal."

"Through sleepless nights and aching days,
This tear, in silence, finds its ways,
A fleeting messenger of peace,
A fleeting kiss that brings release."

"For in that drop, so small, so true,
There's strength that no one ever knew,
A tear, though brief, holds all the sky,
It carries dreams that never die."

"It falls and fades into the night,
A trace of sorrow, pure and bright,
Yet in its fall, it leaves behind,
A softer heart, a clearer mind."

"And when it lands, its work is done,
The heart once heavy now undone,
For tears may fall, but hearts will rise,
To seek the sun beyond the skies."

"So, let it fall, this single tear,
For in its fall, there's love sincere,
And with its journey, far and near,
A new dawn comes, to calm the fear."

CHAPTER TWENTY-THREE

* Dear Engineer *

"Dear engineer, with steady hand,
You craft the future, strong and grand.
Through circuits, codes, and beams of steel,
You make the world a dream to feel."

"With every sketch, a vision starts,
You solve the puzzles, mend the parts.
Your mind, a map of endless skies,
You see the world through clever eyes."

"You build the roads and bridges high,
That stretch beneath the endless sky.
You wire the lights, you tune the sound,
In every corner, you're around."

"Through every challenge, you persist,
A quiet genius in the mist.
You innovate, you mend, you steer,
Our hopes and dreams are built by you, dear engineer."

"In every blueprint, every plan,
You weave the future with your hand.
A silent hero, bold and true,

Dear engineer, we honor you."

CHAPTER TWENTY-FOUR

* O My Dear Friends *

"O my dear friends, with hearts so true,
The world is brighter just because of you.
In laughter shared and moments still,
Your kindness paints the world with will."

"Through storm and sun, you've stayed my side,
With every tear, you've been my guide.
The road may twist, the path may bend,
But with you near, I need no end."

"Your voices bring a steady calm,
A soothing balm, a gentle charm.
In times of joy, in times of strife,
You're the melody that fills my life."

"O my dear friends, you light the way,
Through darkest night and brightest day.
The threads we weave, the bonds we hold,
Are treasures more than purest gold."

"Through every trial, every cheer,
You've held me close, you've brought me near.
A friendship like no other known,
A garden where our hearts have grown."

"O my dear friends, how sweet you are,
Like guiding light, like shining star.
The world may change, but one thing stays:
The love we share, through all our days."

"So here's my heart, so full, so free,
A gift to you, my family.
O my dear friends, you'll always be,
A cherished part of who I'm meant to be."

CHAPTER TWENTY-FIVE

* Bound by Borders, Freed by Hope *

*"**Lines** on maps, walls of stone,*
Divide the lands we call our own.
Flags unfurled, yet hearts confined,
Seeking freedom, we're intertwined."

"We're bound by borders, a human divide,
Yet hope ignites where dreams reside.
A shared desire, a common goal,
To heal the fractures, make nations whole."

"Mountains high and oceans wide,
Cannot suppress the will inside.
A spark of courage, a light unseen,
Breaks the chains where walls have been."

"Hope whispers soft, yet steady and strong,
A melody that's traveled long.
It crosses fences, it scales each gate,

Transforming fear, dissolving hate."

"In every heart, a boundless sea,
A yearning for unity's decree.
For though we differ, we're much the same,
Dreams and love by another name."

"The borders fade, the maps turn old,
But hope remains, its stories told.
Bound no longer, we rise as one,
Freed by hope till the work is done."

CHAPTER TWENTY-SIX

* THE WEIGHT OF SADNESS *

"Sadness comes like a quiet storm,
A shadow with no clear form,
It settles in the heart so deep,
Where secrets, fears, and sorrows sleep."

"It whispers soft, but fills the air,
A weight unseen, yet always there,
It dims the light, it steals the glow,
And leaves a chill that you can't know."

"It's not a tear, it's not a cry,
It's the stillness in the mind's sky,
A pause that stretches, slow, yet sure,
A feeling hard to cleanse, to cure."

"In every moment, there's a trace,
Of something lost, or out of place,
A quiet ache that moves with time,
A silent bell that doesn't chime."

"Sadness speaks without a sound,
It sinks beneath, it wraps around,
It's not the grief of life's great falls,
But the emptiness that silence calls."

"It lingers in the hollow spaces,
In vacant rooms, in quiet faces,
Where laughter once, so freely rang,
Now echoes faint, then fades, then hangs."

"But even sadness wears a mask,
It hides its tears, avoids its task,
For though it pulls the heart apart,
It also teaches where to start."

"For in its depth, we learn to feel,
The pain that shapes, the wounds that heal,
And from its grip, though hard and cold,
We find the warmth of stories told."

"Sadness, though it brings the night,
Will soon give way to morning's light,
For in its pause, we understand,
The strength to rise, to take a stand."

"And though it stays, it does not stay,
Forever locked, forever grey,
For every shadow, every tear,
Will fade, and bring the dawn more near."

CHAPTER TWENTY-SEVEN

* Threads of Existence *

"***Life** is a river, wild and free,*
Winding through valleys, reaching the sea.
A dance of moments, both joy and pain,
A fleeting sun, a sudden rain."

"*It's the laughter shared, the tears that fall,*
The rise from failure, standing tall.
A fragile thread, yet strong and deep,
A dream that wakes, a vow we keep."

"*Life is a puzzle, a curious art,*
A mystery solved by the human heart.
Each piece a story, a step, a scar,
Guided by hope, our guiding star."

"*It's in the silence, the roar, the song,*
In every soul, we all belong.
A fleeting breath, a sacred flame,
Forever changing, yet always the same."

"So live with courage, love, and grace,
Embrace each moment, every face.
For life is a gift, a fleeting stay,
A precious journey, come what may."

CHAPTER TWENTY-EIGHT

* INDIA, A DREAM REALIZED *

"In the heart of the ancient land,
Where rivers whispered tales of sand,
A new dawn breaks with golden light,
India rises, bold and bright."

"From fields once bare, to cities grand,
Technology's touch, a steady hand.
Steel and stone now pierce the skies,
As progress blooms and hope flies high."

"The villages hum with silent pride,
As children's dreams no longer hide.
The roads are paved with future's grace,
As India strides in every space."

"The winds of change, they sweep the air,
A nation's spirit, bold and rare.
In every field, in every mind,
A vision shared, a dream entwined."

"From ancient arts to modern mind,
We carry both, in strength combined.
A tapestry of old and new,
In every thread, the nation grew."

"The heart beats fast, the pulse is strong,
The world will hear our vibrant song.
India, now, is full of grace,
A land that leads, a shining place."

CHAPTER TWENTY-NINE

* Shadows of the State *

*"**In** corridors where whispers tread,*
A power looms, unseen, unsaid.
Behind the veil, where secrets keep,
The shadows of the state run deep."

"They move in silence, they watch, they bind,
Threads of control, unmarked, unsigned.
A labyrinth of laws, a cloak of might,
Blurring the line of wrong and right."

"Promises glimmer like fleeting gold,
Yet truth is bartered, stories sold.
In the quiet, behind closed doors,
Decisions ripple to distant shores."

"Who holds the strings? Who plays the tune?
Beneath the sun, or the pale-faced moon?
A people's cry, a leader's guise,
A web of power shrouds the skies."

"But shadows cannot forever stay,
The dawn must rise, the night must sway.
The truth will out, the light will spread,
And justice wake where fear once tread."

"For though the state may cast its shade,
Hope endures, unbowed, unafraid.
A voice will rise, a spark ignite,
To challenge the shadows, reclaim the light."

CHAPTER THIRTY

* Rise of the Common Voice *

"A murmur in the silent air,
A spark that rises everywhere.
In crowded streets and quiet towns,
The common voice begins to sound."

"Once drowned beneath the weight of power,
It gathers strength with every hour.
Each word a seed, each shout a flame,
Calling for justice, naming the blame."

"No gilded thrones, no crowns of pride,
Can stop the tide that swells outside.
For truth is borne on humble tongues,
In songs of old and those yet sung."

"The farmer's hands, the worker's cry,
The dreams that neither fade nor die,
Together forge a mighty stand,
To claim what's theirs across the land."

"It echoes high, it rumbles low,
A force that leaders come to know.
The walls they build begin to shake,
For every heart is wide awake."

"This is the rise, the voice of all,
A reckoning, a clarion call.
The common voice, long kept apart,
Now weaves its power from heart to heart."

CHAPTER THIRTY-ONE

* THREADS OF LIBERTY *

"***Woven** fine, with care and might,*
Threads of liberty catch the light.
Through years of struggle, war, and peace,
They carry hope that will not cease."

"*A patchwork quilt, both torn and mended,*
By hands of those who never pretended,
That freedom's price was ever small—
They gave their all, they gave their call."

"*Each thread a voice, each stitch a fight,*
For justice born in darkest night.
Bound by courage, sewn with grace,
A timeless bond no force can erase."

"*Yet liberty's cloth is fragile still,*
Tugged by greed, pulled by will.
It frays where apathy takes its place,
And fear seeks power in empty space."

"But hearts awake, the needle sways,
The threads grow strong through brighter days.
Together bound, we weave anew,
A world where dreams can all come true."

"These threads of liberty, soft yet strong,
Sing the anthem where we belong.
Forever stitched in time and space,
A banner held by every race."

CHAPTER THIRTY-TWO

* Of Power and Promises *

*"**Power** stands on lofty thrones,*
Crowned in whispers, forged in stones.
A gleaming scepter, a solemn vow,
Yet beneath the gold, do they know how?"

"Promises bloom like springtime flowers,
Spoken loud in fleeting hours.
But as seasons turn and winds grow cold,
Do those petals wither, their beauty sold?"

"Power commands, it bends, it breaks,
A tool for good or the mask it takes.
Promises echo, hollow or true,
A bridge to hope or chains anew."

"What is power, if not a trust,
To lift the weary, be fair and just?
What are promises, if not a guide,
To light the path where truth may hide?"

"Oh, to wield the power with care,
To honor the words beyond the air.
For in the hearts of those who dream,
Lies the weight of every scheme."

"Of power and promises, let us choose,
Not to deceive, not to abuse.
For power fades, and words remain,
Carved in hearts like a lasting flame."

"May we build with hands sincere,
A future bright, a world held dear.
Where power uplifts, and promises shine,
A legacy crafted, yours and mine."

CHAPTER THIRTY-THREE

* We, The Forgotten *

*"**We** are the whispers in the wind,*
The stories lost, the lives rescinded.
We built the roads, we tilled the soil,
Yet fade away in shadows of toil."

"Our names are etched in fleeting sand,
Erased by time's unyielding hand.
We are the hands that shaped the stone,
But left no mark to call our own."

"We sang the songs, we lit the fire,
Dreamed of more, dared to aspire.
Yet in the pages, blank and bare,
Our voices vanish into air."

"But though we're hidden, we remain,
The unseen threads in history's chain.
In every triumph, every rise,
Lies the sweat of those unseen by eyes."

"We, the forgotten, quiet and small,
Are the roots that hold the tallest wall.
The world may overlook our part,
But we endure in every heart."

"For in the echoes, in the dust,
Lives the essence of our trust.
That though forgotten, we have sown,
The seeds from which all greatness has grown."

"Remember us, the silent ones,
The countless daughters, nameless sons.
We are the foundation, steady and true,
The past unseen that carries you."

CHAPTER THIRTY-FOUR

* A NATION'S PULSE *

"***Beneath*** *the soil, beneath the stone,*
Beats a rhythm all its own.
A nation's pulse, steadfast and true,
A cadence born of me and you."

"*It thrums in fields where farmers sow,*
In rivers where the currents flow.
It hums through cities, bold and bright,
In quiet hearts that dream at night."

"*Through trials faced and battles fought,*
In lessons learned, in freedom sought.
It carries scars, it bears the weight,
Yet rises strong, it does not wait."

"*A nation's pulse is not just pride,*
But the hands that build, the tears that cried.
It's the voice of many, the will to strive,
The bond that keeps its soul alive."

"*It's found in the laughter of children at play,*
In the hopes of tomorrow, the strength of today.
It's justice served and truth embraced,

The light that shines in every face."

"So let us honor the pulse that binds,
A symphony of hearts, of lives, of minds.
For a nation thrives when its people believe,
In the power of unity, the dreams they weave."

"A nation's pulse, a timeless song,
Beating within us, forever strong.
Through every chapter, through every stage,
It writes its story on history's page."

CHAPTER THIRTY-FIVE

* PANCH PRAN *

"In the heart, a rhythm stirs
Fine scared winds, the souls song blurs
Each breath, a prayer, s silent vow
Panch pran guides us here and now."

*"**Prana** the life force , ever flows*
A river of energy that forever grows
It fills the mind, the body, the soul
Breathing balance, making us whole."

*"**Apana** descending,rooted in the earth*
Grounding our spirit , giving re birth
It flows in a clock,deep and profound
A steady current , a healing sound."

*"**Samana** the equalizer ,calm and bright*
It balance within day and night.
Digesting the food ,the thoughts,the strife
It nurtures harmony,sustaining life."

*"**Udana** raising an upward climb*
Raising our spirit to realm sublime
It creates our voice,our wisdom to share

A force of ascension , beyond all care."

"__Vyana__ the circulator,boundless,free
It spread thought out across land and sea
A force of energy in each and every vein
Uniting us all,breaking every chain."

"Five winds,one breath, endless stream
Giving us through the material of dream
Through joy and sorrow ,through raise and fall
Panch pran calls , us awaken of all."

CHAPTER THIRTY-SIX

* Beneath the Banner *

"***Beneath** the banner, colors fly,*
Promises painted against the sky.
Words like thunder, loud and clear,
Yet silence echoes what we fear."

"*A pledge of justice, voices cry,*
But whispers of truth often die.
Beneath the banner, power plays,
Shadows linger in the blaze."

"*Hands extended, deals unfold,*
Dreams exchanged for fleeting gold.
The people wait, their hopes on fire,
For leaders bound to something higher."

"*Beneath the banner, a fragile thread,*
Between the living and the dead.
A trust betrayed, a vow renewed,
A cycle turning, ever pursued."

"What lies beneath? A beating heart?
Or walls of greed that tear apart?
The banner waves, yet all must see,
True change begins with you and me."

CHAPTER THIRTY-SEVEN

* BEYOND THE BALLOT *

*"**Beyond** the ballot, a nation breathes,*
In whispered hopes and tangled wreaths.
Not just the ink that marks the choice,
But dreams ignited in the people's voice."

"A paper cast, a fleeting mark,
Yet shadows linger in the dark.
The walls of power, the halls of greed,
Should serve the soil, not sow the seed."

"A leader's worth is not the throne,
But deeds that heal, not leave us torn.
For justice thrives in open light,
Not shrouded deals in sleepless nights."

"Beyond the vote, the duty stays,
To guard the truth in countless ways.
A citizen's strength, the nation's spine,
Together we rise, a fate divine."

"No banners waved, no slogans screamed,
Can mend the cracks where lies have gleamed.
It's action bold, not empty cheer,
That steers the helm when storms appear."

"Beyond the ballot lies the test,
Of honor's weight and virtue's quest.
Not power claimed, but trust maintained,
For nations prosper where love remains."

"So cast your choice, but don't forget,
The journey's long, the goal unmet.
Beyond the ballot, change takes root,
When hearts unite to seek the truth."

CHAPTER THIRTY-EIGHT

* Sweet Home *

"A place where laughter fills the air,
And gentle winds curl through the chair.
Where walls embrace and hearths still glow,
A home where love is all we know."

"The kitchen hums a quiet tune,
As sunlight spills in afternoon.
The windows open to the sky,
Where dreams take flight and time goes by."

"Beneath the roof, the hearts align,
Through ups and downs, they intertwine.
A refuge built on trust and grace,
Where every soul finds its own place."

"The garden blooms with colors bright,
And every corner feels just right.
In rooms that echo joy and cheer,
Sweet home is where the heart draws near."

"No grand design, no polished gold,
Just warmth and care that's pure, untold.
For in this space, with every part,

Lies the quiet beat of a loving heart."

"So simple, yet it holds the key,
To all that makes us truly free.
Sweet home is where we find our start,
A sacred place to call our heart."

CHAPTER THIRTY-NINE

* LAST FRIEND OF LIFE *

"***When*** *all have left, and silence falls,*
And shadows stretch on empty walls,
One voice remains, soft yet true,
A friend who's stayed, who never flew."

"*Through tears and smiles, they've seen it all,*
The rise, the slip, the bitter fall.
With tender hands, they've caught the cry,
And held the heart that feared to die."

"*No promises, no empty words,*
Just quiet strength when nothing stirs.
In moments dark, when hope feels far,
They shine, a dim and steady star."

"*The world may change, the seasons flee,*
Yet in their gaze, you'll always be free.
Not bound by time, nor worn by age,
They're with you still, beyond the cage."

"A last friend isn't one to leave,
But stays to heal, and to believe.
They're there in moments late at night,
Whispering peace, when fear takes flight."

"In their embrace, the world turns kind,
A soft reminder in the mind.
For when the end draws near, you'll find,
The last friend's love is intertwined."

"And as you step into the night,
They walk with you, a guiding light.
For in the heart, they never stray,
The last friend of life will always stay."

CHAPTER FORTY

* Fragments of a Dream *

*"**In** the quiet of a restless night,*
Whispers of a dream take flight,
Flickering like a fading star,
Dancing just beyond the far."

"pieces scattered in the air,
Fragments of a vision rare,
A moment's hope, a fleeting sigh,
Lost before the morning sky."

"A face, a place, a feeling warm,
Yet tangled in the storm's alarm,
Each fragment calls, yet none are whole,
Like pieces of a broken soul."

"Time slips through the fingers tight,
As dreams dissolve in the early light,
Yet still they linger, soft and bright,
A memory that fades from sight."

*"In the silence, they remain,
Fragments of a dream, a distant strain,
A story unfinished, but still it gleams,
A lifetime etched in scattered dreams."*

CHAPTER FORTY-ONE

* Unwritten Stories of the Virtual Age *

*“**Beneath** the glow of a screen-lit face,*
We live our lives in a silent space.
Words unspoken, yet often heard,
In the hum of a digital world, unheard.”

“Through pixels, we reach across the void,
In endless loops, we’re both seen and destroyed.
Emotions typed with a careful hand,
Shifting, drifting, no longer land.”

“Stories born with every click,
But fading fast, too fleeting, quick.
We write our lives on virtual pages,
Unseen chapters in hidden cages.”

“We are the authors, yet unknown,
In this realm where seeds are sown.
No ink, no paper, no spoken sound,

Yet stories echo all around."

"The faces change, the names do too,
But the essence of us remains so true.
In every heart, a tale to share,
Lost in the ether, floating in air."

"Unwritten stories of this age,
Captured on a digital stage.
A saga of lives in fragments cast,
On screens that flicker, and moments passed."

"In the virtual space, we are all known,
Yet never touched, always alone.
Unwritten, untold, and yet so vast,
The stories of the future, the ghosts of the past."

CHAPTER FORTY-TWO

* Flickering Moments in Time *

"***Like*** *fireflies in the velvet night,*
Moments flicker, soft and bright.
A fleeting glow, a whispered rhyme,
These fragile threads of fleeting time."

"*A laugh, a tear, a glance, a sigh,*
They bloom and fade as hours fly by.
Captured briefly in memory's hold,
Then slip away, both warm and cold."

"*The ticking hands, a steady beat,*
Yet every moment feels bittersweet.
Each one unique, yet hard to define,
A mosaic of flickering moments in time."

"*A child's first step, the last embrace,*
Echoes etched in time's vast space.
Their light may wane, but still they stay,
Guiding us on in their quiet way."

"We chase, we grasp, yet they evade,
Shadows of life, both bright and staid.
But in their shimmer, truths align—
Life is but flickering moments in time."

"Let us treasure the spark before it's gone,
For every moment sings its song.
A fleeting gift, a rhythm sublime,
These flickering moments in endless time."

CHAPTER FORTY-THREE

* Pixelated Dreams and Broken Realities *

*"**In** the glow of screens, I weave my night,*
A pixelated dream, a world of light.
Where colors dance and shadows fade,
A realm of wonder my hands have made."

"Each click, a star, each tap, a stream,
I craft my fate in this fleeting dream.
Yet whispers echo from the seams,
"Beware, beware of broken dreams.""

"For in the haze of neon skies,
Lie fractured truths and veiled goodbyes.
A fragile hope, a mirrored hue,
Reality twists where pixels grew."

"The lines blur thin between the two,
What's false, what's real, what's truly you?
A shattered screen, a splintered heart,

Where virtual ends and life must start."

"But even in the jagged glass,
I find a light, a spark to grasp.
For broken things can still redeem,
A clearer path, a stronger beam."

"So I embrace this world, both flawed and true,
In pixelated dreams, I see what's new.
Through broken realities, I will rise,
A dreamer still beneath the skies."

CHAPTER FORTY-FOUR

* Chasing Tomorrow in the Clouded Sky *

*"**Beneath** a sky of endless gray,*
We chase the dawn of another day,
The clouds weave dreams, both soft and wide,
A future where our hopes reside."

"In whispers lost among the breeze,
We seek tomorrow through the trees,
Unseen, it lingers just ahead,
A promise in the mist, unsaid."

"The sun may hide, the stars may fade,
But we march on, undeterred, unafraid,
For in the haze, there's something clear,
A vision born from doubt and fear."

"Through shifting skies, we rise and fall,
Each step a story, a whispered call,
Chasing tomorrow, we learn to see

That in the clouds, we find the key."

"So let the storms rage, let the winds blow,
With every gust, our hearts will grow,
For in this dance of hope and flight,
We chase tomorrow through the night."

CHAPTER FORTY-FIVE

* Plastic Hearts in a Fragile World *

*"**In** a fragile world where whispers break,*
We wear plastic hearts, for safety's sake.
Molded smiles, polished to shine,
Hiding the cracks we call divine."

"The oceans weep in muted tones,
Beneath the weight of synthetic stones.
Forests echo with silent pleas,
As progress sweeps through ancient trees."

"We trade the raw for the refined,
Covering truth in a glossy bind.
Yet the fragile world, it sees it all,
Hears every creak, feels every fall."

"Our hearts beat on, though veiled in fear,
Afraid to feel, to shed a tear.
But what's a heart that doesn't break?
A hollow echo, a cold mistake."

"Oh, let us cast these shells away,
Embrace the fragile, come what may.
For only hearts unbound, unmade,
Can heal the scars our hands have laid."

"The world may tremble, but it will mend,
If plastic hearts choose to transcend.
To love, to break, to truly feel
A fragile world, a heart of steel."

CHAPTER FORTY-SIX

* THE PRICE OF STARDUST *

"**We** *reached for stars with trembling hands,*
Dreaming of skies and unmarked lands.
A wish on stardust, a whispered plea,
To own the vast, eternal sea."

"*But stars don't give without a cost,*
For every gain, something is lost.
The glow we chased, so bright, so near,
Burned away what we held dear."

"*We traded forests for golden skies,*
And silenced oceans for dreams that rise.
The air grew thin, the nights too cold,
The stories faded, left untold."

"*The stardust shimmered, a fleeting flame,*
A beauty earned in sorrow's name.
Yet as we stood on cosmic shores,
We felt the ache of closed doors."

"For what is stardust in the hand,
When roots are gone from the land?
A fleeting touch, a hollow gain,
A spark alight in endless pain."

"So let us treasure the ground we tread,
The skies above, the rivers ahead.
For stardust shines, but at a price
The cost of wonder, a paradise."

CHAPTER FORTY-SEVEN

* The Algorithm of Emotions *

"***Beneath** the glow of a screen's soft hue,*
A world unfolds, both false and true.
An algorithm hums, its rhythm tight,
Mapping hearts in ones and bytes."

"*It learns our fears, it knows our dreams,*
Threads through our lives in endless streams.
A calculated dance, precise, unkind,
Sorting the chaos of the mind."

"*But can it feel the autumn breeze,*
Or hear the whispers in the trees?
Does it know the weight of a tear,
Or the trembling touch when love is near?"

"*It mirrors joy, it mimics pain,*
A faceless ghost in a digital chain.
Yet what it lacks, we hold inside
A spark of soul, a human guide."

"For emotions aren't just data points,
They're boundless seas, not rigid joints.
No line of code, no neural plot,
Can touch the depth of what we've got."

"So let it learn, and let it grow,
But never let the heart forego
The beauty found in imperfection,
Beyond the algorithm's detection."

"We are more than patterns, clicks, and trends,
We're the pulse that no machine transcends.
In this world of logic, steel, and streams,
Emotions thrive in untamed dreams."

CHAPTER FORTY-EIGHT

* CLOUDS OF MEMORY *

"**The** *clouds of memory drift and fade,*
A shifting tapestry time has made.
Soft and fleeting, yet deeply sown,
They carry whispers of all I've known."

"*A laughter lost, a tear once shed,*
Echoes linger of words unsaid.
Faces blur in the misty haze,
But their warmth remains in countless ways."

"*Some clouds are light, a tender glow,*
A sunny past I still long to know.
Others are heavy, dark with rain,
Pouring out the weight of pain."

"*Yet in their dance across my skies,*
Each cloud a piece of life implies.
The love I felt, the paths I've crossed,
The dreams I chased, the ones I lost."

"They paint the dawn, they veil the night,
Shifting shadows, borrowed light.
And though they fade, as clouds must do,
They leave behind a deeper hue."

"For memories aren't meant to stay,
They drift, they scatter, then slip away.
But their essence clings, like a gentle breeze,
A timeless song through endless seas."

"So let the clouds roll where they will,
They shape my heart, they guide it still.
And in their passing, I see anew
The beauty of a life I drew."

CHAPTER FORTY-NINE

* ARTIFICIAL HORIZONS *

*"**We** chase the line where earth meets sky,*
A crafted dream, a human lie.
Not born of nature's gentle hand,
But forged in glass, by our command."

"A horizon framed by neon lights,
Guiding ships through endless nights.
It bends and tilts, yet stays in place,
A tethered truth in a boundless space."

"But what of skies no man has drawn,
Where stars still sing to greet the dawn?
Do we forget, in our design,
The untamed world that lies behind?"

"These lines we trace, precise and clear,
Anchor us when we feel fear.
But they can't hold the weight of dreams,
Nor quench the thirst of rushing streams."

"Artificial, yet strangely real,
They offer balance we can feel.
A modern wonder, a clever art,
But cannot mend a fractured heart."

"For life itself is wild and vast,
A compass spinning, shadows cast.
No fixed horizon, no steady line,
Just endless paths through space and time."

"So as we soar through skies unknown,
Let's not forget what roots have grown.
For artificial horizons may guide our flight,
But only truth gives lasting light."

CHAPTER FIFTY

* Fragments of a Virtual Dawn *

*"**The** night recedes, its shadows thin,*
As screens alight and dreams begin.
A virtual dawn, a pixelled hue,
Where mornings feel both old and new."

"Fragments flicker, bright and stark,
Pieces of life in a digital arc.
A message sent, a moment shared,
Connections made, yet hearts ensnared."

"The sun outside begins to rise,
But we are lost in glowing skies.
A thousand faces, a nameless throng,
Where silence hums, yet feels so wrong."

"Do we still hear the sparrow's song?
Or see the light where we belong?
This dawn we crafted, byte by byte,
Fills the void but dims the light."

"Yet within these shards of endless streams,
Lie whispers of forgotten dreams.
A chance to bridge, a chance to bind,
The scattered souls we've left behind."

"For every fragment, broken, small,
Can build a world to hold us all.
If only we could look beyond,
And weave together what's been torn."

"A virtual dawn, both gift and snare,
Reflects the truth of what we dare.
To seek connection, near or far,
Yet long for life as real as stars."

CHAPTER FIFTY-ONE

Rewriting Tomorrow's Song

"**We** *stand on the edge of a shifting dawn,*
Where echoes of yesterday are barely drawn.
The future hums with a silent grace,
A rhythm unseen, yet we feel its trace."

"*In the heart of chaos, a melody grows,*
A tune unwritten, where no one knows.
With each step forward, we carve a beat,
Out of the silence, where past and present meet."

"*The song of tomorrow is still in our hands,*
Woven from dreams and shifting sands.
We rewrite the notes, we shape the chords,
As the world spins round, we find our words."

"*A song not of sorrow, nor joy alone,*
But of all we carry, the seeds we've sown.
Tomorrow is waiting, its voice untold,

But we sing it now, with hearts bold."

"We rewrite the future, one verse at a time,
With every heartbeat, with every rhyme.
The song of tomorrow, we'll make it ours,
A symphony born from the hope that powers."

About The Author

SUBHASMITA PANDA

I'm Subhasmita Panda a second year student of Bachelor of Technology . I was born in the year of 2005. After I was born from my mother's womb and brought up by my mother, when I slowly started to know the world, then my thoughts and dreams of becoming a poet were guarding in my mind.

With the blessings of God and the help of my father, I continued to move forward and My father and mother continued to help and cooperate with me. After that, at the age of 18, I discovered a book and wanted to become a role model for people, and my dream came true. As well as being a poet, I am also a good painter who has gained recognition by participating in competitions

across the country and abroad and got certificate and madals from National and International level also.
With a background in engineering, I approache my writing with a unique perspective,merging creativity with analytical thinking. This blend allows me to craft compelling stories that resonate deeply with readers, encouraging them to reflect on my own experiences and emotions. When I'm not writing or immersed in my studies, I enjoy painting, exploring nature, and engaging in literary discussions with fellow aspiring authors. believes in the importance of community and collaboration in the creative process.

I look forward to continuing my journey as a writer, sharing my stories, and inspiring others to find my voices, I hope that my work not only entertains but also sparks conversations that lead to understanding and empathy, At last I have so much inspiration for the next generation, and if they continue to make their own wishes and dreams such a myth, they may all be left behind but the mother who gave birth to them and the father who brought them up can never go away. I am already known as the poet of another book named as " **CHRONICLE CHIMES** " . A part from this my hobbies are Anchoring, Reading novels, puzzle solving ,

I'm a passionate author and poet, celebrated for my unique ability to weave profound emotions and thoughts into words. My book, Embrace of Thought, is a beautiful compilation of poetry that delves deep into the human experience, exploring themes of love, loss, hope, and introspection. Each poem in the collection resonates with readers, offering a gentle yet powerful embrace of emotions and a window into the soul.

My writing style is both eloquent and heartfelt, reflecting my keen observation of life and the world around me. As an author, I seek to inspire, heal, and connect with readers through my evocative use of language and imagery. Embrace of Thought is not just a book but a journey of self-discovery and reflection, making it a cherished piece for poetry lovers.

With this debut work, I has firmly established myself as a voice of authenticity and creativity in the literary world. My dedication to craft and my ability to touch hearts through the words make me a promising author to watch in the realm of contemporary poetry.

Key Points Of Life

1) **Embrace Change**:-Life is dynamic, and growth often comes through change. The willingness to adapt can lead to new opportunities and a deeper understanding of oneself.

2)**Seek Purpose** :- A life lived with purpose feels more fulfilling. Whether it's through relationships, work, or personal growth, aligning your actions with your values brings deeper meaning.

3)**Balance is Key**:- In every aspect of life, balance between work and relaxation, giving and receiving, solitude and social time leads to greater harmony and mental clarity.

4) Learn from Struggles :- Challenges are part of the journey. They help build resilience and provide the lessons needed for personal evolution.

5) **Kindness Matters** :- Small acts of kindness can make a big impact. How we treat others shapes our connections and enriches the world around us.

6) **Find Joy in Simplicity** :- Life's beauty often lies in the simple moments—nature, laughter, a quiet evening. These moments bring a sense of peace that material wealth cannot replace.

7) **Time is Precious** : Time is the one thing we cannot get back. Using it thoughtfully, prioritizing what matters, and living in the present enhances the richness of life.

8) **Self-Awareness Leads to Growth** :-Understanding oneself—strengths, weaknesses, desires, and fears—helps guide decisions and fosters deeper connections with others.

9) **Create, Don't Just Consume** :- Life becomes richer when we contribute something meaningful—whether through creativity, problem-solving, or helping others—rather than just consuming what the world offers.

10) **Gratitude Grounds Us** :- Practicing gratitude brings attention to the positive aspects of life. It shifts focus away from what's lacking to what's already abundant.

* Wings Of Gratitude *

"In the cradle of dreams where words take flight,
You've held my heart in pages white.
Each verse a whisper, a silent embrace,
Reflecting a world, a timeless space."

"To every reader, a quiet friend,
Your kindness gives my journey its end.
Each line you trace, each thought you feel,
Transforms my art, makes it real."

"Your hands turned pages, your soul took heed,
Watered the roots of my poet's seed.
Gratitude blooms, a rose in my chest,
For you, who gave my words their best."

"So here's my thanks, in rhythm and rhyme,
For making my thoughts endure through time.
With every poem, a bridge we've built,
From soul to soul, no space for guilt."

"May these pages find you where dreams reside,
A treasure of words to keep by your side.
For you, the reader, this heart does sing,
Thank you for giving my words their wings."

"Gratitude is the quiet light within that turns ordinary moments into miracles and simple joys into treasures."

"Every reader is a poet's muse, transforming silent verses into shared emotions."

"This book is not just the culmination of my thoughts but also the result of the love, support, and encouragement of those around me. Thank you for believing in my words."

"Here, in the embrace of thought, I offer you the simplicity of moments and the complexity of emotions let your mind wander, and may you find meaning in every turn."

www.ingramcontent.com/pod-product-compliance
Lightning Source LLC
LaVergne TN
LVHW091100150826
845673LV00002B/657

* 9 7 9 8 8 9 6 7 3 6 4 3 1 *